# High Tide

Joy Hooton
# High Tide

## Acknowledgements

Some of these poems were published in *The Canberra Times*, *Blast*, and *Conversations* 5/2 (2005).

'His and Hers' won first prize for poetry in 2009 in the Biennial Literary Awards of the Society of Women Writers Victoria Inc.

Many were initially written for meetings of the Pink Rock Poets in Moruya, NSW.

*High Tide*
ISBN 978 1 76041 173 2
Copyright © text Joy Hooton 2016
Cover: photography by Catrina Vignando, design by Fiona Hooton

First published 2016 by
**Ginninderra Press**
PO Box 3461 Port Adelaide 5015 Australia
www.ginninderrapress.com.au

# Contents

| | |
|---|---|
| Season's End | 7 |
| Annunciations | 8 |
| In the Zone | 9 |
| Mercenary | 10 |
| His and Hers | 13 |
| Semantic shiftings | 16 |
| Retired | 17 |
| Answering the Call | 18 |
| Cottage Prints | 20 |
| Play Up! Play Up! | 21 |
| Winter Peak Hour | 23 |
| Coincidence | 24 |
| Coincidence continued | 26 |
| Verdict | 27 |
| Black or White | 28 |
| Wolf Pair | 29 |
| Sunny Side Up | 30 |
| Generational Change | 32 |
| What's in a Name | 34 |
| Great Aunt | 36 |
| Yorkshire Tea | 38 |
| Break Up | 40 |
| Plum Tree | 41 |
| Wintry Mood | 42 |
| In a Dry Season | 44 |
| Cyclamen | 46 |
| Mental Illness | 47 |
| Richmond Gaol | 49 |
| Subway in Kobe | 51 |
| Les Avants (Swizerland) | 53 |

| | |
|---|---|
| Jerusalem | 55 |
| Country Town | 57 |
| Safaga | 59 |
| Buena Vista Café, Law Courts Building, Sydney | 60 |
| Photograph of a hospital ward in 1940 | 62 |
| Agapanthus | 63 |
| Old Dog | 64 |
| Horse | 65 |
| Lizard | 66 |
| Bird Brain | 67 |
| Dolphins | 69 |
| Another Death in Venice: Lodge on James | 70 |
| The Other Side of Silence | 71 |
| Domestic Fires | 73 |
| Portrait of a Girl in a Red Hat | 74 |
| National Poet | 76 |
| Mrs Hawthorne's Headache | 79 |
| Biography of a Celebrated Artist | 80 |
| A rainbow was a warning | 81 |

# Season's End

When beaches no longer echo with
cries of children,
when the annual funfair is packed away,
and the bins swollen with holiday litter
are empty again,
when days steadily shorten,
pouring out their hours as liquid gold,
when the quiet air hangs suspended in blue,
when early frosts shiver the stars,
when Europe's trees start to recall
their natural cycle,
when the sun, lower now and kinder,
lengthens the shadows and sharpens light,
or softens the evening landscape with
a Venetian glow,
then time becomes silky,
silky as water falling through hands.

# Annunciations

Gold hair scarfed by morning sun,
a young girl stands alone,
arrested by a single sheet,
clamorous with meaning,
released just now from the hive
of steel-grey boxes.

Frozen, white face to white face,
one hand grips the potent message,
the other raised to ward off…
what sharp blows of shock?

Streaming by,
the chattering unconscious crowd
eddies round her soundless cries.

Recalling all those painterly annunciations,
posed invariably as dual solitude,
formal tranquillity, suddenly shattered,
I turn aside.

Sooner the bustling world,
the Angel grasping her elbow
at the noisy market,
or, unseen by others,
turning her aside at the family table,
or, resting his wings on the kitchen sink
seizing her hand as she plucks a chicken,
the momentous lodged in dailiness.

# In the Zone

Rare at summer's noon, they can be found
soon after dawn, gaudy as
tropical birds flying silently on
single-minded journeys,
often alone, but sometimes clustered
in swift flocks, as coherent as
Canada geese, bent on unwavering
mysterious missions.

Patricians of the road, helmeted,
goggled and gloved, clad in multi-
radiant silks, and carrying nothing but
abundant bottles of water, they are
oblivious to plebeian commuters,
plunging them unawares into
colourful slipstreams.

Veterans of every Big Ride,
exultant conquerors of hostile hills,
survivors of saddle sores,
importunate cars and furious dogs,
tearing headwinds, blistering
suns and blinding rains,
their winters are warmed by
European summers, when dreams of
yellow jerseys swell their hours of sleep.

At home, they know best the quietness of
morning, long pooling shadows, soft
burr of tyres, birdsong and
a light breeze on the skin.

# Mercenary

Grey and chill as steel, the day
seems hardly leased from night.
Black snow-packed clouds
hold back their icy flakes
as England holds back war.

On edges of the town, glistening
slag heaps slime the land, man-made
mountains, slug-like pyramids.

Beyond them narrow houses,
drab soldiers at attention,
march impassively and blankly
shoulder to shoulder, down
treeless streets, their signs
echoing national victories, and
recalling in this ironic place
those other markers in fields
    fertile with crosses.

A chapel, soot-blackened, shrieks
of hell fire from its wayside hoarding,
and the Bisto Twins smile falsely
above a shop where boarded windows
    complain that nothing sells.

Uncertain of the way, their car
crawls down empty alleys,
their coming an event unwatched,
    unwanted, out of place.

Only Edna waits in her family's kitchen,
tense, excited, wearing
her best green hand-me-down
coat with the fake astrakhan collar.
Barely sixteen and string-thin,
　she is to be their live-in maid.

There beneath a shameless canopy
of her father's long-johns,
they drink strong sugared tea and
counter his satiric summing up of Mother's
fur and Father's three-piece suit.
His delegate, 'the wife', sheet-white
face above black wrapper,
nervously moves table clutter
to sign her child away,
and an infant, trapped in a walker,
hammers furiously with his spoon.

A snarl is enough to change
his tune to muffled snivelling.

Edna, they learn, has other brothers,
glimpsed briefly in the musty passage,
expelled from these formalities.

The exchange complete,
Father sweeps up her
flimsy cardboard case.

Well used to smaller children,
she grasps her new charge by the hand
and steps into the swirling snow.
Intrepid mercenary, setting out for
    foreign parts.

# His and Hers

At some mysterious moment
   in their married life
they had formed an armistice,
dividing their liver-brick semi
   into His and Hers.
His was the shed and a
   single rear bedroom.
Hers the front double,
sitting room and kitchen.
  In the bathroom's
    no-man-land
  a razor strop and shaving brushes
   bristled a challenge to
powder puffs and coloured crystals.

His zone of garden territory
   supported empty rabbit
   hutches and a kennel
once home to long-dead whippet.
Yellowing weeds marked
   his vegie grave.
   Hers facing the street,
was busy with coloured annuals
   and politely smiling daisies.

    Breakfasting on Players,
he cycled daily to the works
    at dawn
returning on the dot at five
   to receive his dinner
      set out for one
   in the cold kitchen.
Evenings the local pub
afforded conversation
      of a sort.
On rare occasions, mainly wintry,
   he could be found
      slumped
   before a flickering screen,
deaf to the clacking protest
   of her needles,
a stranger in her cushioned clutter.

Given the situation, she
could have taken to religion
     or to drink.
Instead she took to bridge,
the Women's Institute and
       knitting.
Skilled in intricacies of Aran
   or multicoloured fair isle,
   she was adept at cards
     long accustomed to having
       an unlucky hand.

It was uncertain which of them
    or both,
  had named their dwelling.

Creaking noisily above the porch,
   the sign, Bricked Inn,
    teased passers-by
  with a dozen possibilities
    of meaning.

  None of them good.

## Semantic shiftings

An unassuming character,
neither black nor red
and certainly not blue.

A serviceable grey,
admirably in tune with the adaptable role
it has come to adopt,
nudging aside outdated, overblown adjectives,
insinuating itself and its antonym
into the neutral lexicon of our times,
happily working in tandem with
the not-so-innocent verb.

A close neighbour of 'seemly',
and once restricted to the trivia
of dress codes and hairstyles,
to drawing room manners,
to the timing of visits and the leaving of cards,
to the correct periods of mourning
and lying in child bed, or to the
arcane strictures of bureaucrats,
the term has spread like a commonplace weed,
invading cultural landscapes
once gardened by that
old-time heavy weight, morality.

At a time when the old biblical words
have lost their currency, if not their meanings
this shifting/shifty qualifier
has morphed to a blanket public utility,
unfailingly appropriate and ready-made.

# Retired

Good for nothing in old age,
they are incongruous white outdoors,
rain-pitted, sun-blasted, waist-
high in summer grasses.

Once the centre of attention,
essential in every season,
their bounty happily plundered,
they are mocked by cries of
feasting seagulls.

Dumped without ceremony
in a line of fellow has-beens,
large and small, jowl by cheek,
a common price has made them
equal in decay.

Bare-headed, rust-ravaged,
they stare vacantly out to sea.

# Answering the Call

Watched month after month by a hostile sun
in a tedious blue sky
the parched land lay brown,
torpid as a lizard in dry reeds,
listening to a single monotonous sound,
the slow pulse of its breath.

If sometimes at nightfall distant rumblings,
like stirring newspaper headlines,
forecast a change,
it was a promise that sunrise
quickly dispelled as a baseless rumour.

Yet when the torrent finally came,
it was unexpected, as sudden
as a shot from an assassin's gun,
battering the doors and windows,
drumming on iron like a prologue to battle,
lashing the trees and grasses, soaking black
the thin flanks of beasts in the paddocks,
filling the dry creeks with khaki waters.

Remembering, the old men shook
their heads and predicted disaster,
flooded houses and farms and broken bridges,
losses of stock and ruined harvests,
perhaps even diseases and deaths.

But the young men would have none of it,
for the rains had dislodged and floated their future,
transforming their lives like the landscape,
with a wash of Europe's soft colours,
and like the swollen rivers steadily
forcing their way through the deserts,
they were drawn away,
fatally drawn away to the open sea.

# Cottage Prints

Granted an hour's holiday from the thankless
dust-grey paddocks, the iron-hot fibro kitchen and
from her menfolk with their thin threads of words,
she idles in the cool shade of Haberdashery and
Drapery, tentatively fingering crisp cotton prints.

Colours frank as early morning birdsong,
clear as spring water, webbed by intricate
traceries of small predictable patterns.
They are clamorous with glimpses of another
kinder, more possibly beautiful time and place.

Afternoon tea of small cakes on a vine-draped terrace,
eggshell blue china and silver cake stand
gleaming on starched white napery,
French windows ajar on blooming vistas,
a village green at late afternoon, shadows
playing over white figures,
children in chintz sunbonnets and lace-edged bloomers,
paddling in sparkling blue pools.

Exquisite images,
they have the tantalising, arrested
quality of still life,
inviting and denying at once.

But time is nudging her elbow.
she hovers as if wavering under the
advances of a secret lover.
Then, headlong, chooses a length of rose-
coloured fabric, recklessly rejecting the grey
serge already stretched out on the counter.

# Play Up! Play Up!

According to Lord Northcliffe,
    writing in 1917,
  the German soldier,
  being largely ignorant
  of football (in particular)
and having an inadequate concept
    (in general)
  of playing the game,
 was fated to be defeated.

Was he thinking, perhaps, of
   Captain W.P. Nevill,
gallant company commander
   of the 8th Surreys,
  and a keen sportsman,
who encouraged his men
   at the Somme
  to start their attack by
  dribbling footballs
towards the enemy lines?

  Nevill's ball looped high
  over no man's land,
before falling neatly into
  the German trenches
  briefly anticipating
his own looped passage
   to the ground.

    Played away,
  and fatally overseen by
  war's ruthless umpire,
it was his own grand final.

  A rough poem, penned
  by the loyal Surreys, recalls
his feat, though he lies forgotten
  in some corner of a
    foreign field.
  Disqualified for life
   from the game
that leaves all other games
     for dead.

# Winter Peak Hour

Furrowing the road,
mindful of morning's
    deadlines,
Canberra's metallic stream
    roars in full flood.
Sharp edges catch and
    bounce
  the sliding sun, and
  sealed in glass
  shadowy shapes
    flit by,
  fish in deep water.

Down in the valley
sculptured office buildings
  watch the clock for
    late arrivals.

  Indifferent,
slender trunks of
    eucalyptus
listen to older, other
    sounds,
watching as green grey
    lichens
map the stealthy rocks,
  and spiders wait
   for warmer air to
      hide
   their deadly, icy
   traceries.

# Coincidence

One November day in 1780 Luigi Galvani, physician, anatomist and physicist, was dissecting numerous fish, birds and frogs. Several frog legs lay on his desk, their nerves exposed by his skilful hand. By chance, his metal knife touched a nerve in one of the legs at the exact moment when a spark was released by his Leyden jar. Galvani could not believe his eyes. The leg muscles contracted. He had discovered that nerves react to electrical impulses. For the first time, using a simple technical device in the form of a conducting knife blade, he had forged a connection between technical and biological material.

   Spark and blade.
does every life know
    for good or ill
such moments of revolution?
   a blind corner,
an unexpected encounter,
   a twist in the path,
    a turned page?

Or, unrecognised,
the moment might
   lie in wait
  for daylight:
a discovered letter,
an intercepted glance,
  a casual word,
   or, simply,
  the mind, musing,
   stumbles
  on the stone
  that set the ripples
  widening.

Casualty-loaded, near-
   missed, co-
   incidents
   are common:
the doomed plane not boarded,
   the speeding car avoided,
the truck's brakes slamming,
   and holding,
inches from a running child.
   Stabbing reminders of
   our common trending.

   A skin soon forms.

# Coincidence continued

Less easy to forget are
history's nuclear moments,
    exploding in lives
too numerous to count.
  What if St Paul had
    changed his mind
about that journey to Damascus?
    Would the vision
  still have sought him out?
  Or, had the fatal bullets,
    ricocheted at Sarajevo,
    missing their targets,
would the destinies of millions
  have escaped determination?

Sterne liked to claim
his quirky, open mind
    drew thoughts
God meant for others.
More strange and true,
  some are brushed
by premonition's feathered
      wings.
A handful singed by
    second sight.

  But, mostly,
chance beats invisibly
on shuttered minds.

# **Verdict**

Opening the door,
one fine morning,
he saw it at once,
squat on the doorstep,
slyly, implacably waiting.
No address for return,
no name on the collar.

Intuition flicked its tail,
striking him by the throat.

He knew then it was meant.

Shocked,
he was not completely surprised,
for weeks he'd felt portents,
straws,
whisperings at nightfall.

Turning inside,
he saw the windows
had suddenly frosted,
foreclosing the future.

# Black or White

Once upon a time,
the past was simpler,
inhabited by people you could freely admire,
or dislike.
Drake, the king of cool,
waiting to finish his game of bowls
while the Armada sped up the English channel.
Charlie, the bonnie prince, more rightfully royal than,
decidedly more romantic than the Georges,
forever fleeing with Flora o'er the sea.
The evil hunchback king
convicted out of court of murdering
his darling nephews in the Tower.

Back in a complicated now,
simplicity's turned treacherous.
Ripped out of fairy story,
new champions and monsters,
black as snow and white as night,
have hijacked legend to
stalk the minds of millions,
while historians revisions
discount or rehabilitate the past.

# Wolf Pair

Sunday evenings as their dogs
fossicked the ground for scents,
and the light steadily leached into shadows,
time used to take them both by the arm
and slow down to a familiar loiter.

It was then that the week was
a wrinkled sheet, they
smoothed and stretched,
end to end and corner to corner,
trying to fold its meaning
into the press of the past.

Or,
walking and talking,
smoothing and folding,
were they really composing,
trying to find again, and play
the singular ground notes,
a harmony that survived
numerous thunderous passages,
and that was theirs.

# Sunny Side Up

I sometimes think of you, this weather
    you love, when the sea,
    frisked by light north-
    easterlies, plays at
      being a tempest,
trimming its weekend waves
    with fine lacy foam.

When, on the sidelines, ebullient
    flags wave bright-coloured
   cheers to their canvas cousins,
puffs of white, breezily scudding
   holiday sailors over their blue
    watery playground.

When gulls, clown and careen,
    tearing the air with
   screams of excitement,
   and sea eagles soar
    over the coast,
   just for the fun of it.

When the sun, released
    for a time from
revealing linings of silver,
beams from a cloudless
      sky.

Sometimes I wish I had only your
　palette of primary colours,
　 red, yellow and blue,
　　painting the day,
　whatever the weather,
　with your high gloss of
　　romance.

# Generational Change

I'm eighteen again and dressing for a ball.
My escort trained in the codes
of the 1950s has sent an orchid.
Small water drops, retrospective metaphors,
glisten on its pale pink petals.

Mother and aunt fuss,
adjusting a sleeve here, a fold there,
and the figure I see in the glass
is me, and not me, a semi-fictional,
almost-glamorous version,
produced by the arts of our local 'salon'.

My aunt's hands, dry and papery,
fasten the orchid to my dress,
my mother's hair, I notice,
as she bends down to pin the hem,
has thinned recently, exposing sections of
white skull-skin under wire-stiff curls.

Their evening will be quiet.

With the patronage of teenage
and in a rare moment of empathy,
I pity the toasting fork by the fire,
the kettle on the hob, the bags of knitting.

Forty years on,
with the grandchildren safely bedded,
and their parents out for the night,
I settle down with a book,
glad not to be at the beginning of it all.

Were they too, perhaps, relieved
when the taxi drew up,
knowing that, at last,
they had time to themselves?

# What's in a Name

Born too early in Empire's last season,
his parents' union well nigh too late,
he was christened Charles Mortimer
by his clerical grandfather and
enrolled in his father's old school.
Later, in view of his passion for engines
his siblings tagged him Tinker.

Enrolled at sixteen in the Midland Bank,
when poverty and gentility were at odds,
he inherited Peter, the bank's historical name
    for juniors

The name like the occupation was his for life.

Faithfully serving behind the counter fifty
weeks in the year, his real mechanic's day
began at night. Brushed and pressed and
happily discarded, pinstriped suit gave way
at seven to grease-stained overalls.
Like an ancient Clydesdale stirred by scents
of youth, the spotless Daimler puttered out
at weekends. In summer huge veteran motor
bikes hugged his suburban driveway, until
leather-helmeted, gauntleted and goggled,
he tore into the twilight.

The war came as a reprieve.

Enrolled in His Majesty's
Air Force, he stepped into wholeness on windswept
aerodromes. Swinging home on rare weekend leaves,
shouldering his service duffel bag, he came
as the squire of mighty warriors.
Lancasters roaring nightly over Germany,
were armoured with his skills.

Peace demobbed him into boredom.
Robbed of his vocation, and poisoned
by His Majesty's tobacco, he was
dead at fifty-two.

Years later, trying to find a distant cousin,
'Tinker's daughter' bridged a gulf where
   Peter sank beyond recall.

# Great Aunt

The youngest of a country vicar's
never-married daughters and missionary sons,
she was, at last, the oldest.

Her brothers weeded out by
war and India,
her sisters felled by one of Hitler's bombs,
she lived alone, exiled in red-brick,
pebble-dash suburbia.

Beyond her garden gate
the indifferent town plunged
noisily towards the 1950s,
but within the clock was paused
at 1910.

Her days as regular as
the *Times* upon her morning doormat,
a fretwork of small rituals
braced her year.
Morning walks across the common,
matins and evensong on Sundays,
formal exchanges every Monday
with her cleaning lady,
a round of charities for those 'less fortunate',
chopped liver for her evil-tempered cat,
patience and the piano after sunset.

Enormous jigsaws gave the winters meaning,
summer twilights found her lingering waist-deep
   in crowds of English flowers.
In every season books her closest friends.

Religion came as easily as breathing,
   simple civility her rock of faith.
Omitting in his teens to write a note of thanks,
my father lost a lifetime's birthday greetings.

At death, she willed him
all her tiny wealth.

# Yorkshire Tea

A friend has given me a packet of Yorkshire tea.

Bracken-dark brew,
best served with yellow-cream
milk straight from the byre,
the flavour's direct as a hill farmer's oaths.

Memory's an outcrop,
solid and sudden as weather-shaped
limestone, rooted in heather.

Cloud-raked and sky-lonely moors
sham infinity, then fold into hillsides,
tethered and walled into sheep-driven pasture
as neatly as days of the week

Gull-screaming cliffs front dark,
wind-crusted seas.
Inland, brown rivers and streams
hum unconcerned songs
down stone-troubled channels.

Leached from antiquity, great churches
and abbeys linger as ghosts in
Blake's green pleasant land.
In the half-light of winter, industry's
cities hope to forget dawn's
clatter of clogs on the cobbles.

Plain-speaking, dry-humoured,
they face, like their houses,
square-on to the weather,
enmity hugged to the heart
as firmly as friendship.

# Break Up

It was after your phone call
that I first noticed a deep
crack etching itself across the

crazed glaze of our jade green
Chinese jar, destroying a
ceramicist's random cob-

webbed art, and insinuating a
more sinister design in the
nature of things, or at least a

more Newtonian conviction of
sequences. How had we missed
the beginnings of breakage, the

singular signs of strain, until the
moment when a jagged cleft
shattered the shining surface
    of your lives?

# Plum Tree

Every summer, the tree,
  rooted in patience,
    waits
   as the child,
  less patiently,
 watches and waits
 for the moment of ultimate
 ripeness, for the annual
  dark red epiphany.

Down the hill at noon,
office workers, briefly
escaping tyranny of files
and abandoning their
  cool tall towers,
    pause,
arrested as the sharp
   hot light
wavers into pastoral.

  Sweet red plums,
harvested from a child's
   rough billy cart
  recall the lazy taste of
brown-armed, freckled summers
beyond the frontiers of officed adulthood.

# Wintry Mood

In the inward season,
mind squirrels thoughts
summer-hoarded, careless.
  Turned thrifty,
  a cool light sharpens
    expectation.
  But a grey film
  brought by the radio's
    news of maiming,
    killing, dying
has overlaid the familiar
    face of home.

At work night-long,
white winter's pestilence
  has ravaged morning.
  Short-lived, inevitable
    as other empires
    and as forgetful of
    carnage,
it may be gone by noon,
    saving a few, dark
      colonies.

Mist-folded gum trees
have camouflaged themselves
　in military fatigues
　into the paddocks.
　Pinoaks, trembling
　withered leaves,
　　are tattered
　regimental banners.

　A group of wattles,
emblems of sunny youth,
　bloom witless-golden,
　and distant hills,
　a pasteboard backdrop
　　painted blue,
　have lost their
　once-authority.

# In a Dry Season

Watering the plants at evening
    in lonely reverie,
      when an old bird,
   confident to the point of
      familiarity,
dropped in to perch at an
      intimate angle,
leaned his sharp black beak
knowingly in my direction,
    and fixed my glance
with his own bright bead
    of an eye.

Time and water streamed together:

Seconds fused as water drops,
   pouring and dissolving,
   dissolving and pouring,
   with neutral necessity
    into a parched,
    indifferent earth.

Washed down cold tides of
    nothingness,
bird and I were wrecked together
   on a blue ice floe of heartless
     loveliness, until

a sudden avian necessity
   recalled him,
  and swooping down
to snatch a deft late supper,
   returned us both to
   commonplace.

# Cyclamen

Lacking the studied arrogance of orchids,
the sad associations of lilies,
or the yellowing poetry of daffodils,
they rely on a perfect accord
of crystalline pink with
deep velvety green,
on shoots of clustering blossoms
as spirited as champagne bubbles at a wedding.

Above all,
unlike their cut-off colleagues
on the promise of an enduring relationship.

Or, at least,
one that will outlive the greys of winter.

Every year incorrigible,
envious of their obvious happiness with friends,
I fall prey to their professions.

And every year
after a brief burst of passion
and not long after they have left the public
spotlight of a florist's shop,
they lose interest
as rapidly as celebrities in the tabloids,
scandalously abandoning their blossoms
and curling the leaves of their green bed
in a disgust as showy as Melba's,
until the inevitable grubby, hurried divorce
and another relationship
bites the dust.

# Mental Illness

We wait above ground.

   Stone teeth guard
cavernous black mouth.
   Stepping closer,
a chill wind sears our bones.

Who would have thought
such snarls, such serpentine
     windings
curled invisibly beneath
    our feet.

   Listening intently
we can hear rumblings,
    whisperings
and, perhaps, a cry.
We call his name again
   and again,
   but the wind felts out ears.
We have thrown him the rope
   corded with love.
Can he catch it and
   keep hold?
Or will it snag on a rock
   and unravel?
Will the creatures of his
   dark labyrinth
    permit him to leave?

Blocked from entering, we
are like the families of miners
    waiting for news
    after an explosion.

We fear fearing the worst.

# Richmond Gaol

Lavender bursts blue
   against the grey,
and large daisies raise
innocent yellow smiles
   towards the light.
Bees, searching the promised heads,
   thrumm happily.
Sun mellows the rough stony face,
   and two women sit,
downcast and motionless
beneath an almond tree.

Once over the worn-away step,
   bone-chilling,
   mind-numbing,
   heart-wrenching,
    coffin-cells.

Each one a tiny link
   forged
in history's chain
of human cruelty.

Six by three, these narrow walls
 once gripped pincer-tight
   a single, sentient
   breathing body.

Foretaste of the grave,
   frigid in winter,
as good as twelve feet down,
the burial gifts a bucket
  and an iron frame,
leg-irons for ornament.

Sometimes madness, or better,
   a true death
  brought freedom.

  Outside once more,
  in sunlight of today,
  a woman looks up:
'We sit here in their memory.'

# Subway in Kobe

Mid-afternoon
and the languid
   carriages
wait for the hour
when their fish
  will swarm.
Three single suits
  (one m, two f)
and an aged pair
keep shaded silence.

In drops a girl
  like a stone.

Large cowboy hat askew,
  brief leather skirt,
   edged with lace,
black fishnet stockings,
and western boots with heels
   like skewers.
She's wired for sound.

   Her ripples spread.

The wife, perturbed, whispers
  behind a hand.
Her spouse, nose wrinkling, politely
  scans the ceiling (and the girl).
  A suit twitches his paper.
   Eyes meet askance
    in tensed reserve.

Watching her striding
towards the escalator,
   the centre of
   averted eyes,
she's a fish from the tropics,
    plunged into
cold grey northern waters.

# Les Avants (Swizerland)

Immense and starkly arrogant,
self-important, self-sufficient
mountains grip the sky to loom
   their lofty whiteness.

Big is all they know.

But down the valley
new green slopes hug their
quiet velvet and half-leaved beeches
mingle their sweet limes with
   naked sycamores.

At foot, delicate bells of snowdrops
stretch tenderly from heavy soil
and fields of early narcissus
breathe out their heavy scent.

Into the warming air
of Europe's spring
a bird ascends his lusty song.

How many generations,
   lost to all remembering,
   has this land owned?
Their dues are written still
in stone and hedge and furrow.

   Towards evening,
small bands of tired soldiers
struggle through the village

Young, red-faced conscripts
    from the towns,
loaded with heavy packs and rifles
    they're a common sight.

Invading avalanche,
war's imperial big,
perpetual in mind
    in common.

# Jerusalem

Surprisingly smaller than we had expected,
this holy city of sacrifice,
atonement and redemption,
this place of multiple mythic meanings,
millennial visions and apocalyptic fervour,
was also surprisingly mundane
on the day of our visit.

A tourist destination, the city had set aside
conflicting claims of religions and
their disturbing aura of violence,
as believers and non-believers jostled
each other cheerfully in the narrow alleys.

At the Wailing Wall, below the Rock,
place of ritual killings from beyond
the bronze age,
a handful of orthodox Jews
was praying as vendors
in the crowded square
spruiked their souvenirs,
and the sun shone on and on,
sweetly and quietly.

But later on that day, in the same place,
after the tourist coaches had left,
a Jew in traditional dress
was taken for a terrorist and
shot dead by a sniper,
after he called out *Allahu Akbah*

And a day or two later, there were
reports of yet another Western soldier
killed in Afghanistan by those
of a different religious conviction.

Sacred victims, scapegoat heroes.

# Country Town

Two centuries of history have marked
this country town more than most.
Driving in from the west, down a narrow
road fringed with poplars,
you'd swear you were in Europe.
In the main street, broad as a
Paris boulevard, years have
receded like a tide, bleaching
the bones of a thriving past.
At weekends the bakeries are thronged
as travellers pass through to the coast,
but on wintry nights when
not even a brown dog stirs and
the only human face belongs to
a war memorial's traditional soldier,
frost, wind and silence seem
to have the town to themselves.

But surfaces mislead.

Some distance from the western edge of town,
and left by design or chance
when the highway was put through,
a massive rock,
barely contained by the shoulder, and
one side cut sheer as a pane of glass,
watches the road.

Pressed into unofficial service as a billboard,
and freshly painted for every message,
at a hidden time,
by unknown hands or hand,
this natural memorial of the living
blazes into every passing windscreen
glad tidings of the local young.

# Safaga

Safaga sprawls in the sun,
meaningless jumble of mean concrete
blocks littering the shore of a sparkling
blue-green sea. Behind, looming
brown and implacable, range after range of
desolate, serrated mountains
knife the sky.
Beyond lie Luxor, Valley of the Kings
and the Temple of Karnak.

Drawn like flies to a picnic,
as incongruous as our enormous vessel,
line after line of shining coaches
have docked with a purpose.

Tethered on board by circumstance, I watch
as crowds swarm down the gangplanks.

Only a handful of passengers remains.

Self-pity triggers a distant pungent memory.

I am at school again, a crisp
Yorkshire morning and a holiday weekend,
watching alone from an upper window
as a convoy of shining cars cruise
down the wide driveway,
where my luckier fellows are waiting,
certain of liberation.

## Buena Vista Café, Law Courts Building, Sydney

Fourteen storeys up
   a bird's-eye view.
Impressive, muted,
    impersonal,
the gleaming city's self
engrossed in dreams of
   steel and glass,
reduced to vastness.

Inside the view is lost to sight
    and air is fogged with
      urgency.

Law has rolled up his sleeves
   and motley groups,
packed tight as sheep at shearing
   are huddled,
anxiously conferring with his menials,
   senior and junior counsel,
     solicitors and clerks.

The day, perhaps more anxiously
   awaited than birth or wedding,
   has come at last.
For plaintiff and defendant,
   innocent or guilty,
   victim or oppressor,
   swindler or defrauded,
the soothing words of counsel
will soon be tested at the Bar.

Black will give way to Red
and blind uncertain justice
    will be served.

# Photograph of a hospital ward in 1940

A line of single beds,
vacant but expectant,
identical as soldiers on parade,
wait in sepia silence.

Anchoring the beds and
making thin and wavering
their polished presences,
the floor is a dark gleaming pool.

At the burnished heads,
stiff and resolute,
stand white pillows and bolsters,
sheets are turned down at
their regimented length,
corners sharply mitred with
geometrical precision.

Waiting in the wings,
veiled and starched,
there will be Sister and
her infantry of nurses.

War has not yet dispensed
its single good,
the wonder drugs,
if held at bay for this instant,
in the fall of a camera's shutter,
the old enemies.

# Agapanthus

Conspicuously immigrant, and as brightly
blue and white as Greece's national flag,
(no doubt honouring the derivation of their name
agape = love and anthos = flower),
they were in fact seeded, like others,
beyond the seas and, like others,
have struck firm roots in foreign soil.

Timing their flowering to the festive season,
and their colours to the ocean's waves,
they add, for some, a touch of Californian flavour
to our native green-brown coasts.

For others, though, their migrant class and
natural bent of over-breeding,
infuriate,
leading to calls for their addition
to the list of National Pests,
or perhaps the use of borer moths
to facilitate their cleansing.

Native or alien,
weed or plant,
embedded binaries
mirroring the common bent
of mind.

## Old Dog

Ritual of settling done,
she stretches out the pain,
head a flattened cube,
old bones drawing
heat from sun-warmed
    stone.

  Taut and true, life's
a single-threaded cord,
plumbed to a few known
   touchstones,
    not values,
   not even beliefs,
not the human handicap of
    choice.

Enviable on occasion
the grace given to animals
to live a simpler equation,
redefining 'brutish' and 'short'.

# Horse

Flaunting his long, frisky banner,
    flaming his mane,
      black horse gallops to
        yellow-bright,
         sap-surging,
          dew-shining
           morning.

Midday a long streak of black silk
    spread flat on green pasture,
      flanks glisten and soak
        in gluttonous sun.

  Nightfall a shy ghost,
   edging at shadows,
    white blaze
    hovering uneasily
     above his bucket
     like a query.

# Lizard

Faster than eye-blink
he flickers over grass.
Then, curled and small-coiled
lies fast-lidded,
fused to hot stone.

Dreaming deep down
beyond the fringe of thought.
Stilled energy,
assuming torpor.

Daytime incidents,
eye-blinks of memory
flicker across mind.
Then, fuse in deep sleep to
night-time's stirring stories.

# Bird Brain

In his familiar rainbow boiler suit
he is perched on the rail
outside our window,
watching as avidly as any
birdwatcher from a hide
these clumsy, wingless,
featherless creatures.

One of a team of two,
    first and last,
and secondly one of a flock,
he is monogamous and masterly,
a builder of nests and regular father
    of fledglings,
driving many of his larger cousins
    away from the grain
      in a single swoop.

As sure of his role and purpose
in the nature of things
    as a pope,
self-doubt will never ruffle
the soft down on his breast.

Legal codes are foreign
    to his thinking
   but laws he lives by
are sewn as tightly into his heart
    as into plume on his body.

What he knows is small,
but like the hard grain he seeks
   real and rounded
     and enough.

# Dolphins

Happily,
they were here again this morning.

I caught them not a moment too soon,
sun silvered streaks riffling the blue.

Elemental play,
more sparkling than early birdsong,
glistening knife-blades falling sheer.

Lost,
impossible innocence.

Born wild in lawless country,
more alien, weird and dangerous
than fantasies of science fiction,
their salty fathomings
mock our littoral imaginings.

Yet hints of human likeness,
signs of family and community
make a language of relation,
drifting us closer,
while surging apart.

# Another Death in Venice: Lodge on James

Of course,
it could not possibly be true,
a case of authorial licence
one writer's take on another.

But, still.

Drawn to Venice by her suicide,
as he was not by her life,
by her valid emotional claims
and by their rare congruence,
of minds, that is,
he hires a gondola
early one cold, dark morning,
intending to drown her long white dresses
in the canal.

Unweighted, however,
they refuse to sink,
flapping and ballooning eerily to the surface,
enclosing him and his craft in
a relentless freezing embrace.

In a life
so finely ordered and contained,
serving only the demands of a difficult art,
was her death, in fact,
an eruption of raw horror,
ballooning itself without warning
into the mind?

# The Other Side of Silence

'If we had a keen vision and feeling of all ordinary human life, it would be like hearing the grass grow and the squirrel's heart beat, and we should die of that roar which lies on the other side of silence.' – George Eliot, *Middlemarch*

It's hard to imagine George Eliot having time for poetry,
fitting it in between the years of hard labour
   on *Romola* and *Daniel Deronda*.
Nevertheless it's a fact that she made a few
attempts at it, drawing on the same impure well
   of childhood watering the *Mill*.

It failed to take, however.

An elephant attempting ballet
   was the general opinion.

Taking to prose and Victorian
   density of clauses
   as naturally as a cat to milk,
she needed sentences as wide as crinolines,
phrases as intricately carved as great-
great-grandmother's parlour furniture,
words like meliorism, humanity and piety,
   as awkward out of context as
   Royal Doulton at a barbecue.

That creature, wise omniscience, required
vast acres of arable and populated
　　land for range.
Set to graze on poetry's sparse pasture,
　　tethered by rhyme,
it foundered as sententious platitude.

But within the novel's ample score,
　she found her proper scope.

Empathy, sounding the ground-note
　in symphonies of orchestrated
　moral destinies, rising and falling
in crescendo and sad diminuendo,
fashioned a fresh prose-poem equation,
echoing cries from that unimaginable roar
　the other side of silence.

# Domestic Fires

As Mrs Gaskell observed,
a bright fire in the grate
meant a great deal to Charlotte
forever stirring the embers
to vermilion intensity,
obsessively sweeping the tiles
free of coal dust,
no doubt excluding with
heavy draperies, the
desolate moors,
as she studied the troubled
face of Rochester,
half-lit to Byronic grandeur
by the blaze.

Incandescent with fury,
she set a match at last
to his sultan's ardour
settling him down,
maimed and half-blind,
a domestic pet
at the family hearth.

# Portrait of a Girl in a Red Hat

The identity of *Girl in a Red Hat* is unknown, but it is possible that she is the key to the failed relationship, which some historians maintain influenced the dark paintings of his last decades.

Four centuries on
her smile wins you over,
just as it is said to have captured him
   before the crisis.

Did he perhaps tell her to lilt her chin,
lifting her perfectly formed mouth
out of the shade of the brilliant hat,
so that her eyes shone with a darker radiance
   from within its depth?

Or was the posture characteristic,
a frank signature of identity,
neither bold nor arrogant,
contrived nor self-conscious,
a glance that met you confidently,
    and warmly,
   more than halfway.

Was it he who chose
such an indulgent prop to her beauty?
Not just red but
unblushingly scarlet,
casting its brim in accord with her cheek line,
flirting a feather with a luxuriant ringlet,
blatantly playing the role of foil
to skin's creamy whiteness.

Present and absent,
anonymous and intimate,
elusive and fixed,
she fascinates her observers
four centuries on.

# National Poet

   Rattling back from
back of Bourke, third class,
courtesy of a mob of cattle,
bound for Sydney's abattoirs,
the country's sad immensity
   maddens him with its
     monotony.

   The same sun-seared scrub,
    doggedly brown,
  dull familiar of that
    year-long epic
  humping his bluey,
bending endlessly towards sky-
  oppressed horizons,
heat-white or blanket-grey.

  Beyond the tracks,
  scenes slip by at random,
like stale, unhappy memories
    of childhood.
  A swagman's camp,
square of calico stretched
  across a horizontal stick,
  rags steaming by his fire.
Funeral line of sheep straggles
  across the darkening flat.
   Near derelict shanty,
tethers several wretched horses.

Watching, the glass throws
    back his face,
catching for a moment the
   dark soulful eyes
Longstaff will record.

  Stunted and starved,
the land, like his youth,
  is rich with promise
    of failure.

Hope, a hollow wood heap,
will feed only a brief fire
   of passion.
Mateship its surrogate,
  more a matter of
necessity and pathos than
   celebration.
  Beer dulls, then
  drowns his senses.

Over a century on,
the Bush he hated
  and created
holds him tight in
  mythic grip.
Composted deep in
  culture's garden,
he's familiar as Phar Lap,
applied to streets and suburbs,
plaques and parks and playgrounds.
Novels, plays and festivals
   celebrate his name.
  Anthologised and analysed,
  scholarship dissects him, and
biographers squabble noisily, while
engraved upon a nation's currency,
  he's folded into wallets.

# Mrs Hawthorne's Headache

When Hawthorne read the end of *The Scarlet Letter* to his wife, 'it broke her heart and sent her to bed with a grievous headache'.

His ancestors were men of substance,
and convictions,
high-hatted, sable-cloaked,
and Bible–carrying,
never doubting that cruelty
was God-given and a mandatory mercy.

Cringing at the memory of their careers,
he changed his name,
though they monitored his own
irregular profession
from beyond the grave.

Meddlers to a man,
they intervened
when at last he wrote the famous book,
twisting the telling,
quenching her scarlet, passionate energy,
acclaimed by generations of his readers.

She escaped the whipping,
or worse,
great great grandad would have wanted,
condemned instead to solitary confinement
in grim, authentic Salem.

A normally phlegmatic man,
he could barely read his closure,
without great gusts of sobbing.

# Biography of a Celebrated Artist

Privately he scorned what was made of it,
his life. How his past was ransacked
for clues. How ten years of scholarship
reverently mined his slender archive
for a history as circumstantial as
a legal brief. Banal chronology,
measuring the days as if time,
dropped grain by grain through
a pedant's glass, could tell the tale.

Undiscovered, that head-strong, heart-
flung summer. Barely twenty, he'd crammed
another twenty into weeks. Passion,
    torture and betrayal,
enough to feed the work of thirty years.

As for painting's core, the mind's rough
journey, daily wrestle of hand and eye,
soaring exhilaration to festering despair,
failure's raw anguish…
and the mystery, sweet mystery of the given,
    sweet fugitive grace.

Of this nothing was glimpsed.

Enough the work itself,
agent of its own destiny.

# A rainbow was a warning

A rainbow was a warning
we should have heeded.

Drawn by the naked calm of spotted eucalypts,
we plunged deeply into their green silence.
Tender tendrils of delicious maidenhair
licked our boots, though
sharp admonishments of tree ferns
scraped our arms.

Disturbed,
leaf mould flung its rotting fragrance,
and on occasion huge termite boulders,
blunt reminders, blocked our way,
but undeterred we hurried on.

Till rain,
sharp and unexpected as shrapnel,
struck our faces.
Too late we remembered
long rocky passages, impenetrable cliffs
the rising tide.

Blinded, unnerved by a sudden
scramble of tracks, lit in a flash
of lightning, we turned at random.

Hemmed in by the glistening bush,
our trail trudged us onward,
dogged and truculent as lost infantry,
following manic directions,
up rocky slopes, through
stony creeks and down
steep gullies.

But suddenly the track relented,
broadening and promising a future, and
we were led like prodigal children
into familiar country,
until at last, stretching below us,
the friendly beach,
the westerly sun lighting the waves,
and the windows of home.

www.ingramcontent.com/pod-product-compliance
Lightning Source LLC
Chambersburg PA
CBHW062146100526
44589CB00014B/1707